23 DEC 1994
31 MAR 1995
30 JUN 1995
22 DEC 1995
PROJECT
30 DEC 1998

ABERDEENSHIRE
LIBRARY &
INFORMATION SERVICES
ABERDEENSHIRE COUNCIL
WITHDRAWN
FROM LIBRARY

GRAMPIAN
REGION
6054   J665
SCHOOLS'
LIBRARY
SERVICE

Books should be returned on or before the last date stamped above.

CW01543516

Oil Rig

A Cherrytree Book

Designed and produced by
A S Publishing

First published 1989
by Cherrytree Press Ltd
a subsidiary of
The Chivers Company Ltd
Windsor Bridge Road
Bath, Avon BA2 3AX

Copyright © Cherrytree Press Ltd 1989

British Library Cataloguing in Publication Data

Graham, Alison
   To an oil rig.
   1. Offshore natural gas & petroleum industries.
   Offshore platforms
   I. Title   II. Reed, Neil
   III. Series
   622'.338

   ISBN 0-7451-5041-1

Printed in Italy by Imago Publishing Ltd

All rights reserved. No part of this publication may be reproduced, stored in a retrieval system, or transmitted, in any form or by any means without the prior permission in writing of the publisher, nor be otherwise circulated in any form of binding or cover other than that in which it is published and without a similar condition including this condition being imposed on the subsequent purchaser.

Let's go to an
Oil Rig

By Alison Graham
Illustrated by Neil Reed

CHERRYTREE BOOKS

The petrol we use in our cars comes from oil.

Oil comes from under the ground. It has to be pumped up. On land people drill oil wells to reach the oil.

Some oil is found under the sea. To reach it, people have to build an oil rig.

An oil rig is a man-made island in the sea. It has long legs that stand on the sea bed. The oil is in the rocks under the ground.

People live on the oil rig and drill down to reach the oil.

Let's go and see how they do it.

The oil rig is a long, long way from the land. It takes a long time to get to it by boat. Sometimes the sea is so rough that ships cannot reach the rig.

The people who work on the rig fly there in a helicopter. The supplies they need go by ship.

A supply ship stays near the rig all the time. Sometimes the weather is too bad for the helicopter to land on the oil rig. It lands on the ship instead.

supply ship

Our helicopter reaches the oil rig safely. On the rig, we meet the director. He is in charge of the rig and its crew of workers.

He tells us all about the oil rig and about the oil it is drilling for. He gives us a Fact File.

You can see the Fact File at the end of this book.

rig director

The director tells us how they find the oil under the sea. Some kinds of rocks are more likely to have oil in them than others. When scientists find likely rocks, they send a jack-up barge to drill a test well.

Small boats called tugs tow the barge out to sea. The barge has big legs that stick out of the top. When the barge is in the right place, the legs are lowered until it is standing on the sea bed. Then the crew start drilling.

Sometimes the sea is too deep for a jack-up barge. Its legs would not reach the bottom. Then they use a floating rig. The rig has big air tanks. Chains anchor the rig. They hold it steady while the drill goes down to the sea bed.

semi-submersible rig

anchor chains   drill

In places where the sea is calm, they use a ship to drill the test well. The drill goes through a hole in the bottom of the ship. The ship is good because it can move from place to place. But it cannot stay steady if the sea is rough.

drill bit

The drill looks like a piece of string going down to the sea bed. It is called a drill string. But it is not string. It is a long, strong pipe made of steel.

At the end of it, there is a steel bit. The bit has big steel teeth. They bite into the sea bed.

As the drill bit bites into the rock, the men on the rig have to make the drill longer. They fit new pieces of pipe to the top of the drill.

drillers

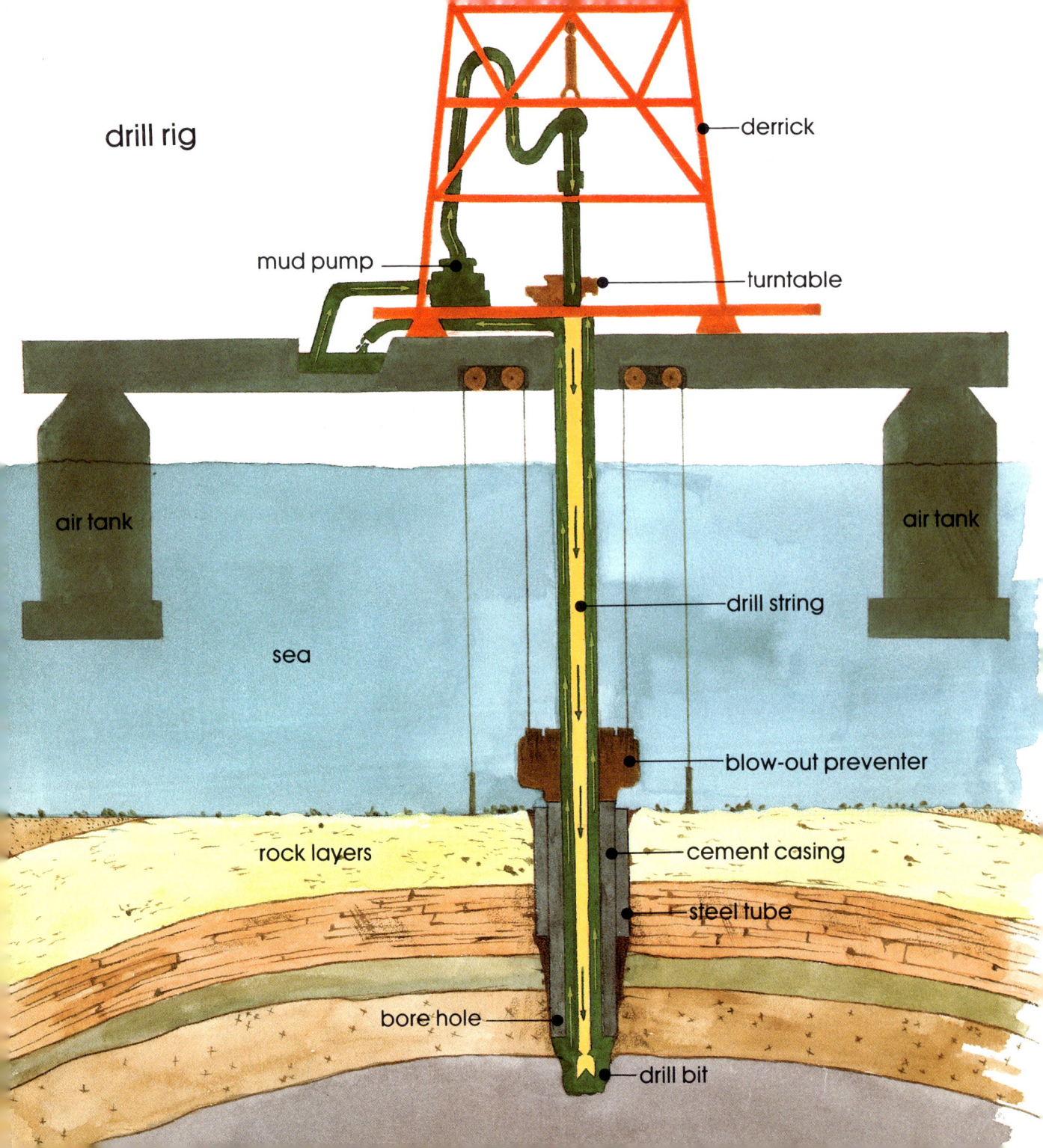

The hole the drill makes is called a bore hole or well. Big steel tubes are cemented into the bore hole to stop it collapsing.

A tall tower on top of the rig holds up the drill. The tower is called the derrick. An engine makes the drill bit turn as it bites the rock. As the bit turns, the broken rock is pushed up the bore hole.

A muddy mixture of oil, water and chemicals is pumped down the pipe. This 'mud' keeps the drill cool and comes back up with the broken rock.

A scientist looks at the bits of rock. He can tell from them whether they are about to strike oil.

The drill bit wears out every few days. Replacing it is a big job. The whole drill string has to be lifted up and unscrewed piece by piece. The drillers fit the new bit. Then they put the pipe back together again. It takes all day to do.

A person called a tool pusher is in charge of the drill. He tells the drillers what to do.

tool pusher

oil gusher

Christmas tree

Everyone wants to strike oil. Nobody wants the thick, sticky oil to gush out of the well.

To stop the oil gushing, the drillers put a cap on the well. It has so many pipes and valves that it looks like a Christmas tree. It is called a Christmas tree. The valves make the oil flow gently through the pipes.

When the oil company knows that there is a lot of oil, they build a big production platform. This is like a drill rig, but bigger.

As well as the drilling equipment, there are places for the workers to live. They may stay on the rig for months at a time.

production platform

The oil platform is a busy place. Drillers and rotary men look after the drill. Other members of the crew called roughnecks and roustabouts look after the deck. They keep it tidy and wash off the slippery oil. They scrape off rust and paint the equipment.

derrickman

deep-sea diver

The derrickman looks after the lifting gear. He has to go high up above the platform. He directs the big cranes that lift the pipes and machinery around.

Deep-sea divers look after the parts of the rig under the sea. Metal rusts quickly in water, so there are often repairs to do.

Once the oil is out of the ground it has to be taken ashore. It is pumped along the sea bed in a long pipeline. On the way it goes through a processing chamber. From there it goes into big storage tanks on the sea bed.

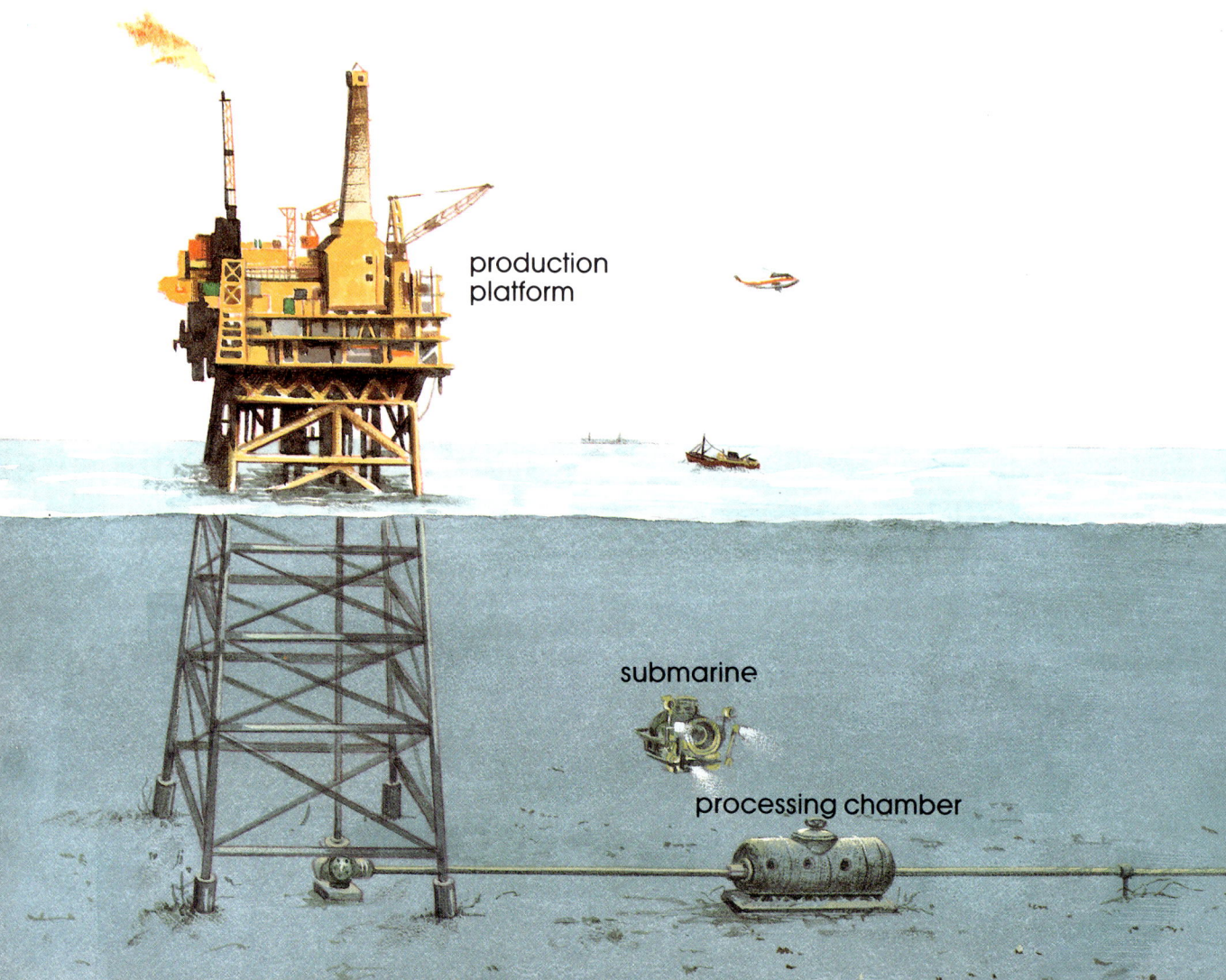

Pipes from the storage tank go up to a buoy that floats on the surface. Oil tankers can pick up oil from the buoy. They cannot load the oil from the platform itself. They are too big to moor alongside.

Other pipelines take the oil all the way to the shore.

Workers travel to and from the underwater equipment in small submarines.

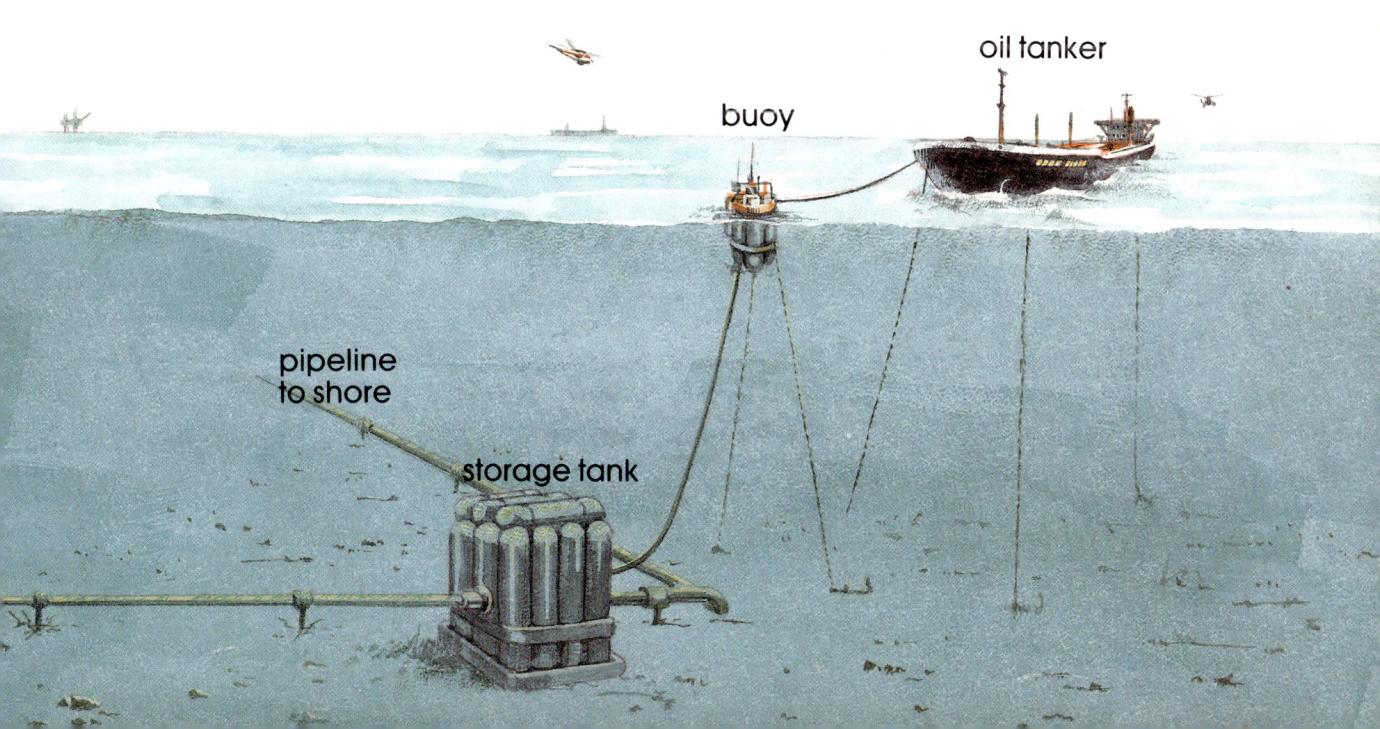

Working on an oil rig is very hard. Most of the crew work twelve hours a day. They are tired when they finish work. They go to their cabins, change out of their working clothes and have a shower.

Working in the cold outdoors makes them hungry.

Food on oil rigs is always good. Meals are free and the workers can eat as much as they like.

After supper they can play cards or snooker in the games room. They can get a book from the library or watch a film or television in the cinema. Life on a rig is like life on a big ship.

Every oil rig has a radio room. This keeps it in touch with the mainland, with other oil rigs and with ships. The public telephone is linked to the radio so that the crew can talk to their families and friends at home.

There is also a computer in the radio room, which is linked to the engines and to all the equipment aboard the rig.

The workers stay on the rigs for at least two weeks. Then it is time for them, like us, to go home.

The helicopter arrives with a new crew. We go aboard with the old crew and fly home. There are so many questions still to ask. See if you can find the answers in the Fact File.

helicopter

Fact File

What is oil?
Oil is a dark sticky liquid. It is sometimes called black gold because it is so valuable. It gives us fuel and lots of other products.

What is it made of?
It is made of the remains of billions and billions and billions of tiny plants and animals that lived in the sea in prehistoric times.

How did the oil form?
The tiny plants and animals were like the ones that live in the sea today. They lived in the shallow water near the sea shore. When they died, their bodies sank to the bottom and decayed.

Sand and mud drifted down

plants and animals magnified 100 times

dead plants and animals

sand and mud

hard rock

and covered their remains. The sand and mud piled up in layers and became very heavy. The weight of the layers above pressed on the ones below. The sand and mud hardened into rock. The plant and animal remains were squeezed into liquid oil or gas. The oil and gas seeped into the ground and was trapped under the rocks. It took hundreds of millions of years for the oil to form.

How do scientists know where to look for oil?

Some rocks have tiny holes in them. Water and oil can seep through the holes. These rocks are called porous rocks. Other rocks are hard. Nothing can flow through them. Oil and water and gas are found in porous rocks between hard rocks. Scientists find the right kind of rock formations in areas that were once covered by seas.

Why does oil burn?
Oil burns because it is the remains of plants and animals. Coal is formed from the remains of prehistoric trees. It also burns well.

Where do you find oil?
You find oil in places all over the world. Much of the oil comes from places that are now deserts. Once the land was covered with seas.

Which scientists know about oil?
Scientists who study rocks are called geologists. They know where to find oil. Chemists know about what oil is made of. Oil engineers know how to get the oil out of the ground.

How much oil is there?
Nobody knows how much oil there is. Every day the world uses 55 million barrels (almost 9000 million litres). Scientists think that we may run out of oil within the next hundred years.

What do we use oil for?
We use oil mostly for fuel. We burn it in our cars and use it to make electricity. We also use it to make hundreds of different things. These are just a few: glue, paint, plastics, dyes, detergents, nylon, foam cushions and even delicate hand cream.

Are there different kinds of oil?
The oil from the ground is called crude oil. It can be separated into different kinds of oil. This happens in a refinery.

How is oil refined?
The crude oil from the well is distilled. It is boiled in a tall furnace. When it boils, it produces vapour like steam from a kettle. The vapour condenses (changes back into liquid) as it cools.

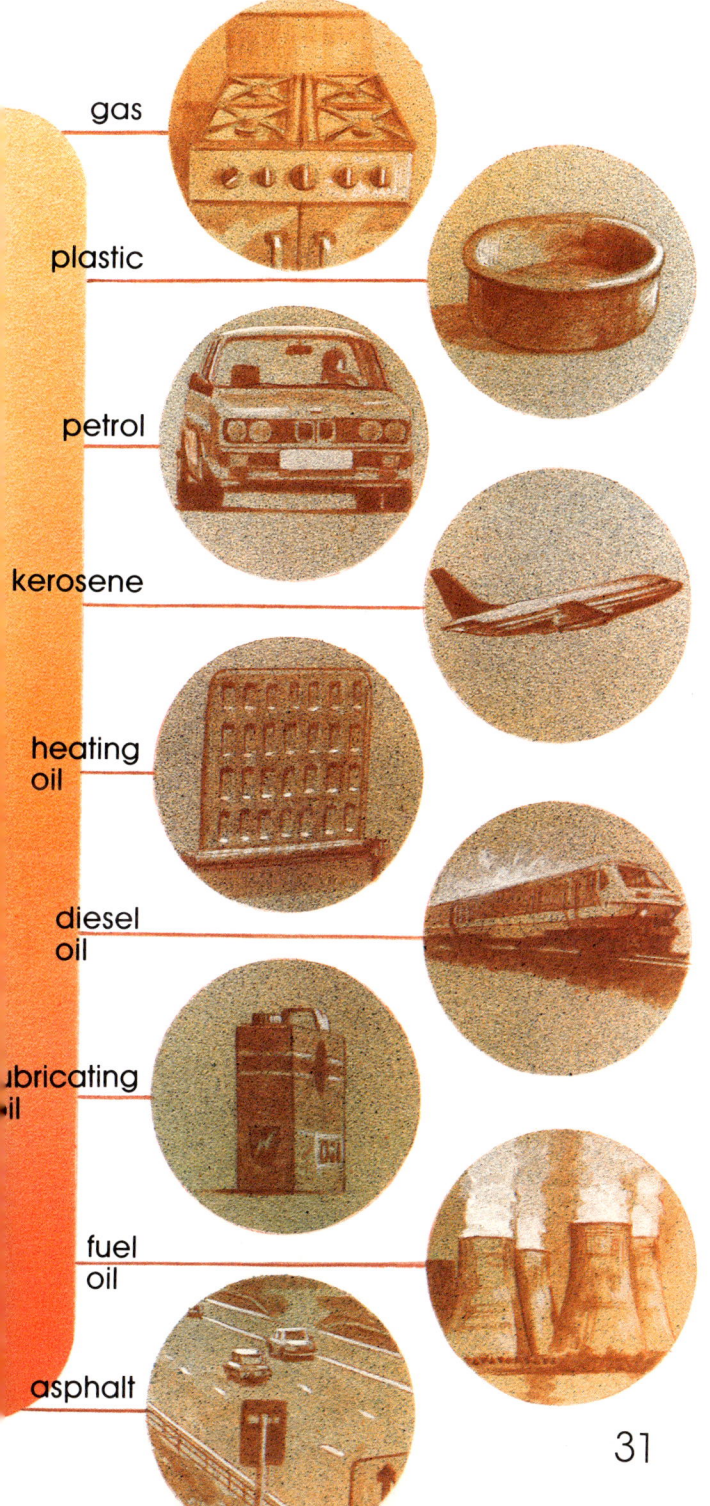

Different parts of the oil condense at different levels. The heaviest parts are at the bottom, the lightest at the top.

What is refined oil used for?

The lightest part of the oil does not condense. It remains as a vapour, or gas. It is used for fuel.

The heaviest part of the oil makes heavy fuel like diesel oil. The thick particles left at the bottom make asphalt which is used to make the surface of roads. Heavy oil is also used to make machinery run smoothly. It oils, or lubricates, the moving parts.

In between the gas and the really heavy oil, there are grades of oil for heating our homes and for burning in power stations to make electricity.

The best oil is used to make kerosene fuel for aeroplanes and petrol for cars.

Index

blow-out preventer 14
bore hole 14, 15
buoy 23

cabins 24
Christmas tree 18, 19
cinema 25
computer 26
cranes 21
crew 8, 24, 26, 27

deck 20
deep-sea diver 21
derrick 14, 15
derrickman 20, 21
drill 10-16, 20
drill bit 12, 14-16
drillers 13, 16, 18, 20
drill rig 14, 18
drill ship 11
drill string 12-14, 16

engines 24

floating rig 10
food 25

games room 25

helicopter 6, 7, 27

jack-up barge 8-10

library 25
lifting gear 21

mud 15
mud pump 14

oil 5, 8, 15, 18, 20, 22, 23
oil company 18
oil platform 20
oil rig 5-8, 15, 24-27 (see also drill rig; production platform)
oil tanker 23
oil well 5, 18
oil workers 8, 18

petrol 5
pipeline 22
production platform 18-22
processing chamber 22

radio room 26
repairs 21
rig director 8
rocks 5, 8, 12, 15
rotary men 20
roughnecks 20
roustabouts 20
scientist 8, 15
semi-submersible rig 10
ship 6, 23, 26
storage tanks 22, 23
submarine 22
supply ship 6

telephone 26

television 25
tool pusher 13, 16
tugs 8, 9
turntable 14

workers 8, 27

Fact File Questions

The answers to these questions are on pages 28-31 and are not included in the index
What is oil?
What is it made of?
How did the oil form?
How do scientists know where to look for oil?
Why does oil burn?
Where do you find oil?
Which scientists know about oil?
How much oil is there?
What do we use oil for?
Are there different kinds of oil?
How is oil refined?
What is refined oil used for?